For a young generation of dreamers:
Please help those dreams come true – B.M.

For J.O. and J.S. for living the Dream.
And especially for Siena, with love – B.W.

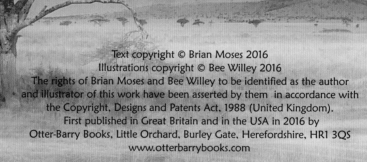

Text copyright © Brian Moses 2016
Illustrations copyright © Bee Willey 2016
The rights of Brian Moses and Bee Willey to be identified as the author
and illustrator of this work have been asserted by them in accordance with
the Copyright, Designs and Patents Act, 1988 (United Kingdom).
First published in Great Britain and in the USA in 2016 by
Otter-Barry Books, Little Orchard, Burley Gate, Herefordshire, HR1 3QS
www.otterbarrybooks.com

A catalogue record for this book is available from the British Library.

ISBN 978-1-91095-959-6

Illustrated with mixed media

Set in Malandra

Printed in China

9 8 7 6 5 4 3 2 1

DREAMER

Saving Our Wild World

Written by Brian Moses
Illustrated by Bee Willey

Otter-Barry BOOKS

Once I had a dream,
a special dream,
a dream about our world.

I dreamt I was a whale...
and no hunters
chased after me.

I dreamt I was a seal...
and no one wanted
fur from me.

I dreamt I was a stream...
and nobody
poisoned me.

I dreamt I was a lake...
and no one filled me
with junk.

I dreamt I was a valley...
and no one built
a road across me.

I dreamt I was a rainforest...
and nobody felled
a single tree.

I dreamt I was an elephant...
and nobody stole
my ivory.

I dreamt I was a panda...
and no one took
my territory.

I dreamt I was an island...
and no one ever
discovered me.

I dreamt I was the air...
and nothing
blackened me.

I dreamt I painted a smile
on the face of the Earth
for all to see.

It's Time for Action!

All the animals and wild places in this book need to be protected
and looked after, to save them for the children of the future.
Dream of a better world, and then take action to help save our beautiful planet.

- The wildlife population of the world has declined by 50% since 1970. (WWF)

- There are as few as 3,200 tigers, 1,864 giant panda and 880 mountain gorillas left in the world. (WWF)

- There are only 3,000 blue whales in the world today where once there were 220,000. (Marine Bio.)

- Every 2 seconds an area of forest the size of a football field is destroyed. (WWF)

- Each year 3 times as much junk is dumped into the world's oceans as the weight of fish caught. (Marine Bio.)

Here are some useful websites to get you started:

Helping to save our forests -
The Rainforest Alliance: www.rainforest-alliance.org
The Woodland Trust: www.naturedetectives.org.uk
Planet Ark: www.planetark.com

Helping to save animals and birds -
Worldwide Fund for Nature: www.wwf.org.uk
Royal Society for the Protection of Birds: www.rspb.org.uk
National Geographic Kids: www.kids.nationalgeographic.com

For other ways to help our planet, check out
www.wateraid.org
www.fairtrade.org.uk
www.recyclenow.com
www.greenlivingonline.com

We hope you enjoyed our book, and here's to the future.
Brian Moses and Bee Willey